To:

_____

From:

_____

Date:

_____

5-Minute Bible: 100 Stories & 100 Songs

Published in Nashville, Tennessee, by Tommy Nelson. Tommy Nelson is an imprint of Thomas Nelson. Thomas Nelson is a registered trademark of HarperCollins Christian Publishing, Inc.

Stories written by Stephen Elkins.

Illustrated by Tim O'Connor.

Original song by Stephen Elkins: "I Love Him Better Every D-A-Y."

Songs adapted by Stephen Elkins: "He's Got the Whole Worlds in His Hands," "We Are Climbing Jacob's Ladder," "Donkey Riding," "Be Kind," "Climb Sunshine Mountain," "For Such a Time as This!," "Psalm 23," "When I Am Afraid," "Praise the Lord Together," "I Have Decided to Follow Jesus," "Ask, Seek, and Knock," "The Golden Rule," "What a Mighty Hand," "For God So Loved the World," "He'll Be Walking Across the Water," "Mustard Seed Faith," "I Am the Good Shepherd," "Be a Good Samaritan," "Everybody Ought to Know," "Father, We Thank Thee," "Jesus Loves the Little Children," "Sing Hosanna," "J-E-S-U-S," and "Paul and Silas."

All other songs are in the public domain.

Full song lyrics can be found at www.wonderworkshop.com.

Tommy Nelson titles may be purchased in bulk for educational, business, fund-raising, or sales promotional use. For information, please e-mail SpecialMarkets@ThomasNelson.com.

ISBN-13: 978-0-7180-9764-6

Library of Congress Cataloging-in-Publication Data

Names: Elkins, Stephen, author. | O'Connor, Tim, 1953- illustrator.
Title: 5-minute Bible : 100 stories and songs / created by Stephen Elkins ;
    illustrated by Tim O'Connor.
Other titles: Five-minute Bible
Description: Nashville : Thomas Nelson, 2017.
Identifiers: LCCN 2017007436 | ISBN 9780718097646 (padded hardcover)
Subjects: LCSH: Bible stories, English. | Hymns--Juvenile.
Classification: LCC BS551.3 .E3485 2017 | DDC 220.95/05--dc23 LC
record available at https://lccn.loc.gov/2017007436

Printed in China

17 18 19 20 21 DSC 6 5 4 3 2 1

Mfr: DSC / Shenzhen, China / August 2017 / PO #9442163

ALL NEW MATERIAL
Filling: POLYURETHANE FOAM
REG. NO. MA-46199 (CN)
MADE IN CHINA

5-MINUTE BIBLE

100 STORIES & 100 SONGS

Created by
Stephen Elkins

Illustrated by
Tim O'Connor

A Division of Thomas Nelson Publishers

Contents

A Letter to Parents

Childhood is such an exciting stage of discovery and growth, and there's no greater time to introduce the Bible. Although some complexities of the Bible are too advanced for little ones, simple Bible stories can reveal the truth of God's Word, and those truths will stay with a child for a lifetime. *5-Minute Bible: 100 Stories & 100 Songs* will introduce Bible stories in a simple yet meaningful way.

Each Bible story is written in a kid-friendly style and includes takeaway statements that will help little ones understand and remember God's truth. Paired with each story are Bible songs that will make story time even more fun and memorable. Some songs that are repetitive in nature will include only the first line of the second and third verses to help get you started. Full song lyrics can be found at www.wonderworkshop.com.

So set aside five minutes today to curl up with your little one, and discover amazing Bible stories and songs!

Creation

Genesis 1:1–25

God made everything. When God said, "Let there be light," there was light! He called the light *day* and the dark *night*. That is what God did on the first day. On the second day, God made the sky. On day three, He separated the land from the oceans. Then He made the trees and flowers.

On the fourth day, God made the sun, moon, and stars. On day five, God filled the oceans and lakes with fish. He made all the different types of birds too. On the sixth day, God made all the animals.

God made everything good. But He wasn't finished yet!

God is good.

God made everything good.

I know God is good because of what He made.

He's Got the Whole World in His Hands

He's got the whole world in His hands
He's got the whole world in His hands
He's got the whole world in His hands
He's got the whole world in His hands

He's got the heavens and the earth in His hands
He's got the heavens and the earth in His hands
He's got the heavens and the earth in His hands
He's got the whole world in His hands

Adam and Eve

Genesis 1:26–2:25

On the sixth day of creation, God made the first man. His name was Adam. God also planted a beautiful garden called Eden. The garden was full of trees and plants that made good food for Adam to eat. It was a perfect home with everything he needed.

Then God gave Adam work to do. He was to take care of the garden God had made. Then God said, "It is not good for Adam to be alone. I will make him a helper." So God made a woman. Her name was Eve. Together, Adam and Eve lived in the garden and worshipped God.

God created everything.

God made Adam and Eve.

God made me too!

God Made Me

God made me, God made me
In my Bible book it says that
God made me

God loves me, God loves me
In my Bible book it says that
God loves me

God helps me, God helps me
In my Bible book it says that
God helps me

Temptation for Adam and Eve

Genesis 3:1–6

God said to Adam, "You may eat from every tree in the garden except one." God warned Adam that if he disobeyed, he would die. One day the evil one appeared in the garden in the form of a snake. He was very clever. He found Eve and asked, "Did God really tell you not to eat from any tree in the garden?"

Eve answered, "We cannot eat from the tree in the middle of the garden."

"You will not die," he said. "Try it!"

So Eve looked at the fruit. It looked good to eat. She remembered God's warning. But believing the lie, she took the fruit and ate it. She gave some to Adam too. Adam and Eve disobeyed God.

God always tells the truth, but Adam and Eve did not listen to God.

I will listen to God.

6

Be Careful, Little Eyes, What You See

Oh, be careful, little eyes, what you see
Oh, be careful, little eyes, what you see
For the Father up above is looking down in love
So be careful, little eyes, what you see

Oh, be careful, little ears, what you hear

Oh, be careful, little hands, what you do

Leaving Eden

Genesis 3:8–24

Adam and Eve heard the voice of God calling, "Adam, where are you?"

Adam answered, "We're hiding because we're afraid."

Then God asked, "Adam, did you eat the fruit I told you not to eat?"

Adam answered, "Eve gave me the fruit."

Then God said, "Eve, what have you done?"

She said, "The snake tricked me."

Adam and Eve were ashamed of what they had done. They had disobeyed God. Then God said to the evil one, "You have done a bad thing." God told Adam and Eve, "Now you will have to leave Eden and work very hard." It was a very sad day.

Disobeying God causes trouble.

Adam and Eve disobeyed God and had to leave the garden.

I will obey God and receive His blessings!

Standin' in the Need of Prayer

It's me, it's me, O Lord
Standin' in the need of prayer
It's me, it's me, O Lord
Standin' in the need of prayer

Not my father, not my mother
But it's me, O Lord
Standin' in the need of prayer
Not my sister, not my brother
But it's me, O Lord
Standin' in the need of prayer

Noah Builds the Ark

Genesis 6

Noah was a good man living in a bad time. All the other people had become mean and unkind. They didn't love God at all. All they thought about was doing mean things. That made God very sad.

But Noah and his family loved God. This made God happy. God told Noah to build a big boat called an ark. He said there would be a flood and all the earth would be covered with water. Noah and his family would be safe on the ark. God would send animals to Noah so they could be safe too.

Loving God makes Him happy.

Noah loved God.

I will love God.

Who Built the Ark?

Who built the ark? Noah! Noah!
Who built the ark?
Brother Noah built the ark

Old man Noah built the ark
He built it out of hickory bark
He built it long, both wide and tall
With plenty of room for the large and small

Who built the ark? Noah! Noah!
Who built the ark?
Brother Noah built the ark

Noah's Big Boat

Genesis 7

God brought two of every kind of animal to the ark. In came two cats. Can you find a kitten? In came two giraffes. Can you find a giraffe? Then God closed the door. The thunder crashed. *Boom!* The lightning flashed. *Zoom!* The animals were so afraid! It rained for forty days and forty nights. Floodwaters covered the whole earth.

But Noah's ark floated upon the waves. Up and down went the great big boat. At night Noah could hear the sounds of all the animals. But Noah's family and the animals didn't mind. They were safe in the ark! There were antelope, buffalo, cats, dogs, elephants, and foxes. Can you name some of the other animals aboard Noah's ark?

God keeps us safe.

Noah obeyed God and was saved from the flood!

I will trust God to keep me safe.

Noah's Arky, Arky

The Lord said to Noah:
There's going to be a floody, floody
Lord said to Noah:
There's going to be a floody, floody
Get those children (clap)
Out of the muddy, muddy
Children of the Lord

Noah's Rainbow

Genesis 8–9:17

The rain stopped. Noah sent out a raven, and it kept flying back and forth until the land had dried. Noah then sent a dove, but it couldn't find a perch, so it returned to the ark. A week later, the dove went out again and returned with an olive leaf. And after another week, the dove went out but did not return.

This meant that the land had dried up, so Noah, his family, and all the animals came out of the ark. Noah thanked God for keeping them safe. God put a beautiful rainbow in the sky to show He would never again flood the whole earth. It was a beautiful day!

A rainbow is a sign of God's promise.

Noah thanked God for sending the rainbow.

When I see a rainbow, I will remember God's promises to me.

Praise Him, Praise Him, All Ye Little Children

Praise Him, praise Him
All ye little children
God is love, God is love
Praise Him, praise Him
All ye little children
God is love, God is love

Father Abraham

Genesis 12:1–4; 15:5–6; 21:1–5

One day God spoke to Abraham, "Leave your country and go to a land I will show you. I will bless you and make your family into a great nation." Abraham obeyed God.

One night God told Abraham, "Look at the sky. There are so many stars you cannot count them. Your family will be like the stars. Your family will become so big that you won't be able to count them all." Abraham was puzzled. He and his wife Sarah were very old and had no children. But Abraham believed God. Later, when Abraham was one hundred years old, Sarah had a baby boy, just as God had promised. They named him Isaac.

Nothing is too hard for God.

Abraham believed God.

I will believe what God says.

Father Abraham

Father Abraham had many sons
Many sons had Father Abraham
I am one of them and so are you
So let's all praise the Lord!

Abraham and Isaac

Genesis 22:1–13

Abraham and Sarah loved their son, Isaac. One day God decided to test Abraham to see how much he loved God. God said, "Abraham, take Isaac and give him back to Me." That made Abraham very sad. But he knew he could trust God.

So together, Abraham and Isaac climbed a steep mountain. Isaac said, "Father, I don't understand. Where is the lamb?"

"God will provide," Abraham said.

Suddenly an angel called out, "Abraham! You do not have to give your son back to God. Now God knows you love Him more than anything, even more than your own son. Because you trusted God, you and your family will be blessed more than all people."

God wants us to love Him more than anything.

Abraham loved God and offered to give Isaac to Him.

I will love God more than anything.

Rock-A My Soul

Rock my soul in the bosom of Abraham
Rock my soul in the bosom of Abraham
Rock my soul in the bosom of Abraham
Oh, rock-a my soul!

Too high, can't get over it
Too high, can't get over it
Too high, can't get over it
Gotta go through the door

Too wide, can't get 'round it

Too deep, can't get under it

A Wife for Isaac

Genesis 24:1–22

Isaac grew up. Abraham, Isaac's father, sent his servant to find Isaac a wife. As the servant came to the town, he stopped at a well. He asked God to help him find Isaac a wife: "When the young women come to get water from the well, guide me to Isaac's wife. Let her give me a drink, and then let her offer water for my camels too."

Just then, Rebekah came carrying a water pot. She gave him a drink from her water pot. She said, "Here is water for your camels too." He knew Rebekah was God's choice for Isaac.

God guides those who pray.

Abraham's servant prayed, and God guided him.

I will pray for God to guide me.

He Keeps Me Singing As I Go

There's within my heart a melody
Jesus whispers sweet and low:
Fear not I am with Thee, peace, be still
In all of life's ebb and flow

Jesus, Jesus, Jesus
Sweetest name I know
Fills my every longing
Keeps me singing as I go

Twins for Rebekah

Genesis 25:21–34

Isaac and Rebekah were about to become parents. God told Rebekah her twins would be very different: "One will be stronger than the other. The older brother will serve the younger."

When the babies were born, they were such a blessing. The oldest twin, Esau, was red and hairy. The younger twin, Jacob, had fair hair and smooth skin. Esau grew up to be a skillful hunter. Jacob stayed close to home.

One day Esau came in from hunting and was very hungry. Jacob had just made soup, so Esau asked for some of it. Jacob said that Esau must give him the rights of the firstborn in exchange for the soup. Because Esau did not appreciate his firstborn rights, he traded it for soup. Later Esau served Jacob just as God had said.

Be thankful for God's many blessings.

Rebekah was thankful for Jacob and Esau.

I will have a thankful heart.

Count Your Blessings

Count your blessings
Name them one by one
Count your blessings
See what God has done

Count your blessings
Name them one by one
And it will surprise you
What the Lord has done

Jacob's Ladder

Genesis 28:10–22

Jacob was on a long journey. As night came, he stopped to rest. He used a large stone for a pillow. While he was sleeping, he had a dream. He saw a stairway leading up to heaven. The bottom of the stairway rested on the ground. The angels of God were climbing up and down the stairway. At the top of the stairway was God. He said to Jacob, "I will watch over you. I will be with you wherever you go." And Jacob promised he would trust God.

God watches over us.

Jacob trusted God.

I will trust God to watch over me.

We Are Climbing Jacob's Ladder

We are climbing Jacob's ladder
We are climbing Jacob's ladder
We are climbing Jacob's ladder
Soldiers of the cross

Behold, I am with you and will watch o'er you
Behold, I am with you and will watch o'er you
Behold, I am with you and will watch o'er you
Soldiers of the cross

Joseph's Coat

Genesis 37:1–28

Years passed and Jacob had twelve sons. One day Jacob gave his son Joseph a special coat of many beautiful colors. Jacob did not give his other sons a special coat. Joseph's brothers were very jealous of him. Then God sent Joseph important dreams. Joseph told his brothers about them. Joseph's brothers did not like his dreams and were angry.

One day one of the brothers said, "When Joseph brings our food, let's get rid of him."

"Let's throw him into a pit," another said.

Then they had another idea. They sold Joseph as a slave to some traders. But God took care of Joseph.

God is with us, even in the bad times.

He was with Joseph when his brothers sold him as a slave.

In hard times I know God is with me.

God Will Take Care of You

Don't be upset if bad news comes
God will take care of you
Beneath His shelter of love you'll run
God will take care of you

God will take care of you
Through every day, o'er all the way
He will take care of you
God will take care of you

Joseph Forgives

Genesis 39; 41–45

The traders took Joseph far away to Egypt. But God took care of Joseph. One day Joseph was asked to explain the king's dream to him. The king was so pleased with Joseph's answer that he made Joseph an important leader.

One day all of Joseph's brothers came to Egypt to ask for food. They were afraid when they saw Joseph because they didn't know what he would do to them for selling him. But Joseph forgave his brothers and gave them the food they needed. Then his whole family moved to Egypt. His father, Jacob, was happy to see his son again.

God tells us to forgive others.

Joseph forgave his brothers.

I will forgive others.

Heavenly Sunlight

Walking in sunlight all of my journey
Over the mountains, through the deep vale
Jesus has said, "I'll never forsake thee"
Promise divine that never can fail

Heavenly sunlight, heavenly sunlight
Flooding my soul with glory divine
Hallelujah! I am rejoicing
Singing His praises, Jesus is mine

Baby Moses

Exodus 2:1–10

Jacob's family grew in number. The new king in Egypt did not like them. One day an Israelite woman had a baby boy. Since the king was so mean and wanted to get rid of the baby boys, she hid her baby from him. She made a special basket that would float in water. Carefully, the mother put her baby in the basket. Then she put the basket in the river among the tall grass.

An Egyptian princess saw the basket floating in the water. When she found the baby boy, she loved him. The princess decided to keep the baby. She named him Moses. Moses' sister was watching nearby and said, "I can find a nurse to take care of the baby." And she brought Moses' own mother to care for him. God took care of baby Moses.

God watches over us all.

He kept baby Moses safe.

God watches over me and will keep me safe.

Angels Watchin' Over Me

Day is dyin' in the west
Angels watchin' over me, my Lord
Sleep my child and take your rest
Angels watchin' over me

All night, all day
Angels watchin' over me, my Lord
All night, all day
Angels watchin' over me

The Bush That Wouldn't Burn

Exodus 3:1–10

Moses was once a prince in Egypt. But he broke the law while trying to defend an Israelite slave. So Moses ran far away and became a shepherd.

One day Moses was with his sheep and saw a bush that burned with a brilliant flame. But the bush did not burn up! God spoke from the bush saying, "Moses, take off your sandals. This is holy ground." Then He told Moses, "Go back to Egypt and tell the pharaoh to let My people go free." Soon Moses was on his way to Egypt to do what God said.

God speaks to us through the Bible, other people, and things that happen.

Moses heard God in a burning bush.

I will listen to God's voice and obey Him.

Let My Little Light Shine

This little light of mine, I'm gonna let it shine
This little light of mine, I'm gonna let it shine
This little light of mine, I'm gonna let it shine
Every day, every day, every day in every way
I'm gonna let my little light shine

On a Monday, He gave me the gift of love
On a Tuesday, His peace came down from above
On a Wednesday, He told me just what to say
On a Thursday, He taught me just how to pray
On a Friday, he gave me a little more faith
On a Saturday, He gave me a lot more grace
On a Sunday, He gave me the power divine
To let my little light shine

The Red Sea

Exodus 14

Pharaoh finally let God's people go free. But then he changed his mind and sent his army to capture them. God's people saw Pharaoh's army coming. They had no way of escape. Pharaoh's army was behind them. The sea was before them.

But Moses trusted God. He shouted, "Do not be afraid. God will save you!" Then Moses lifted his staff and the Red Sea parted. God made a road through the middle of the sea! As they reached the other side, God let the water go back, and the army could not go through it. God's people were saved!

God can make a way when there is no way.

God parted the Red Sea for Moses and God's people.

I will trust God to make a way for me!

I Feel Like Traveling On

My heavenly home is bright and fair
I feel like traveling on
No pain nor death can enter there
I feel like traveling on

Yes, I feel like traveling on
I feel like traveling on
My heavenly home is bright and fair
I feel like traveling on

The Lord has been so good to me
I feel like traveling on
Until that blessed home I see
I feel like traveling on

The Ten Commandments

Exodus 20

Moses led the Israelites through the desert. On the way, God told Moses to go to Mount Sinai. Moses went up the mountain alone. There God gave Moses ten important rules to follow. God wrote the Ten Commandments on stone tablets.

A commandment is not something you *might* do. It is something you *must* do. God said these ten rules were to be obeyed. God knew that if the people obeyed the Ten Commandments they would live safe and happy lives.

God's ways are true.

God gave us the Ten Commandments as rules to follow.

I will honor God. I will obey His rules.

This Is My Commandment

This is My commandment
That you love one another
That your joy may be full
This is My commandment
That you love one another
That your joy may be full

That your joy may be full
That your joy may be full
This is My commandment
That you love one another
That your joy may be full

Balaam and the Talking Donkey

Numbers 22

Balaam made a poor choice. A bad king sent his servants to offer Balaam a lot of money if he would say unkind things about the people of God. Balaam took the money and left on his donkey to go with the king's servants.

God was not pleased with Balaam. He sent an angel with a sword to block his way. Balaam didn't see the angel in the road, but his donkey did. Three times the donkey ran off the road. Three times Balaam beat his donkey. God made the donkey speak, "Why did you hit me?" Balaam couldn't believe it—a talking donkey! Then Balaam saw the angel too. He told God he was sorry. God forgave him, and Balaam returned to bless God's people.

God sends helpers to show us His way.

Balaam listened and followed God's direction.

I will listen to people who teach me God's way.

Donkey Riding

It's a miracle, I say
Balaam's donkey spoke that day
Heavenly angel blocked the way
Riding on a donkey

Hey, ho, away we go
Donkey riding, donkey riding
Hey, ho, away we go
Riding on a donkey

Balaam's choice was very bad
He was sorry, he was sad
God forgave him, now he's glad
Riding on a donkey

Promised Land

Deuteronomy 34

Moses and the Israelites had traveled in the desert for forty years. God taught them to trust Him. He taught them to obey. He showed them His power. After years of learning God's lessons, they were ready to enter the Promised Land. Moses did not get to go with them, but God showed him the Promised Land from the top of Mount Nebo.

God blesses those who learn His lessons.

The Israelites were blessed.

I will learn God's lessons and look forward to His blessings.

When the Saints Go Marching In

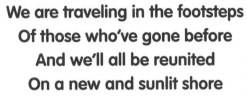

We are traveling in the footsteps
Of those who've gone before
And we'll all be reunited
On a new and sunlit shore

O when the saints go marching in
O when the saints go marching in
Lord, how I want to be in that number
When the saints go marching in

Rahab's Hidden Secret

Joshua 2

Joshua was a brave soldier. He sent two spies into Jericho to find out how his army could defeat the enemy. The spies went to Rahab's house. Rahab had heard about God's power. She wanted to help these men because she knew God was on their side.

The king of Jericho found out that the two spies were in the city. He sent his soldiers to find them. Rahab hid the two spies to help them escape. The soldiers came looking, but they did not find the spies. Because Rahab helped the men, God protected her and her family.

Soldiers in God's army help each other.

Rahab helped the spies and was saved.

I will help God's people.

I'm in the Lord's Army

I may never march in the infantry
Ride in the cavalry, shoot the artillery
I may never zoom o'er the enemy
But I'm in the Lord's army (Yes, sir!)

I'm in the Lord's army (Yes, sir!)
I'm in the Lord's army (Yes, sir!)

I may never march in the infantry
Ride in the cavalry, shoot the artillery
I may never zoom o'er the enemy
But I'm in the Lord's army (Yes, sir!)

Joshua's Battle of Jericho

Joshua 6

The two spies returned to Joshua. They told him that the people of Jericho were afraid. A very tall wall surrounded Jericho. The wall was made of stone. How would they ever get through the wall?

God told Joshua and his army to march around Jericho one time each day for six days. Then on the seventh day, the people were to march around the city seven times. They were to blow the trumpets and shout really loudly. Then the walls of Jericho would come tumbling down! Joshua followed God's instructions, and when the people blew trumpets and shouted, the wall *did* fall down. God's way won the battle.

God's ways are not our ways.

Joshua fought the battle of Jericho God's way and won.

I will do things God's way.

Joshua Fit the Battle

**Joshua fit the battle of Jericho
Jericho, Jericho
Joshua fit the battle of Jericho
And the walls came tumbling down**

Now you may talk about your men of Gideon
You may talk about your men of Saul
But there's none like good ol' Joshua
At the battle of Jericho

Samson

Judges 16

Samson was in big trouble! God had given him a mighty strength. No one could defeat him. But now that strength was gone. As long as Samson obeyed God, his strength remained. But he had not obeyed.

So there he stood, tied between two pillars in the enemy's temple. Then Samson prayed, "Lord, give me strength one more time." Samson's strength returned, and he pushed the pillars down, making the temple roof fall down on the enemy. God answered Samson's prayers and saved His people.

God will give us the strength we need when we ask Him.

Samson prayed for strength, and God supplied it.

I will pray for strength in the Lord.

He Is Lord

He is Lord, He is Lord
He is risen from the dead
And He is Lord
Every knee shall bow
Every tongue confess
That Jesus Christ is Lord

Ruth

Ruth 1–4

Naomi, her husband, and their two sons moved to a faraway land. Her sons married women named Orpah and Ruth. But Naomi's husband and sons died. Naomi was very sad. She wanted to go home to the land of Judah.

Naomi told Orpah and Ruth to go back to their own homes. Orpah did just that, but Ruth loved Naomi and could not leave her. She told Naomi, "Where you go, I will go. Your people will be my people, and your God, my God." So Ruth went with Naomi. Because of her kindness, God blessed Ruth with a husband and children.

God blesses us when we are kind and love one another.

Ruth showed love and kindness to Naomi.

I will show love and kindness to others.

Wherever He Leads, I'll Go

"Take up your cross and follow me"
I heard my Master say
"I gave my life to ransom thee
Surrender your all today"

Wherever He leads, I'll go
Wherever He leads, I'll go
I'll follow my Christ who loves me so
Wherever He leads, I'll go

Hannah's Prayer

1 Samuel 1

Hannah was very sad because she had no children. One day Hannah and her husband went to the temple. Hannah prayed, "Lord, remember me. If You will give me a son, I will give him back to You. When he is old enough, I will bring him back to this temple to serve You."

God heard Hannah's prayer and gave her a baby boy. She named him Samuel. Hannah kept her promise to God. When Samuel was old enough, Hannah took him to the temple. Samuel served the Lord his whole life.

God answers our prayers.

God remembered Hannah's prayers and gave her a son.

When I pray, I know God hears me.

Do Lord

Do Lord, oh, do Lord
Oh, do remember me
Do Lord, oh, do Lord
Oh, do remember me
Do Lord, oh, do Lord
Oh, do remember me
Way beyond the blue

Young Samuel

1 Samuel 3

When Samuel was a young boy, he became God's helper. He lived in the temple with Eli, the priest. One night, Samuel heard a voice call him. He thought it was Eli. Samuel got up and went to Eli. "Here I am," he said. Eli told Samuel he hadn't called him, so Samuel went back to bed.

Again, Samuel heard the voice. And then once more. Eli told Samuel if he heard the voice calling again to say, "Speak, Lord. I am listening."

Soon Samuel heard the voice. This time Samuel answered, "Speak, Lord. I am listening." And God spoke to Samuel. Samuel listened and grew up to be one of God's best helpers.

It is good to listen to God and be His helper.

Samuel was God's helper and heard His voice.

I will listen and be God's helper too!

Now I Lay Me Down to Sleep

To the tune of "Twinkle, Twinkle, Little Star"

Now I lay me down to sleep
I pray the Lord my soul to keep
Keep me safely through the night
And wake me up with morning light
Now I lay me down to sleep
I pray the Lord my soul to keep.

David Praises God

1 Samuel 16:14–23

Saul was the king of Israel. Sometimes Saul would be very sad and grumpy. One of Saul's servants thought that listening to happy music would make Saul feel better. He knew a shepherd boy named David who could play the harp. So the servant sent for David.

David loved to praise God with his music. He came to the palace and played his harp for the king. The king felt much better. Praising God pleases Him and can make anyone feel better!

God is worthy of praise.

David praised God with music to make Saul feel better.

I will praise God too!

Little David, Play on Your Harp

Little David, play on your harp
Hallelu, hallelu
Little David, play on your harp
Hallelu!
Little David, play on your harp
Hallelu, hallelu
Little David, play on your harp
Hallelu!

David Fights Goliath

1 Samuel 17

The Philistine army came to fight God's people. One of the Philistine soldiers was a giant warrior named Goliath. Goliath was over nine feet tall. He wore a suit of armor and carried a heavy spear. Every morning, the giant shouted mean words and made fun of God.

God's people were afraid of Goliath. But David the shepherd boy said, "I'll fight that giant!" David took his slingshot and found five stones. David shouted to Goliath, "You come with a sword and a spear! But I come in the name of God!" David put one stone in his slingshot. *Whizzzz, bonk!* The stone hit Goliath in the forehead. He fell like a big tree. David won! God was on his side.

If God is on our side, we can do great things.

With God's help, David won the battle against Goliath.

If I call on the Lord, He will help me.

Only a Boy Named David

Only a boy named David, only a little sling
Only a boy named David, but he could pray and sing
Only a boy named David, only a rippling brook
Only a boy named David, but five little stones he took

And one little stone went into the sling
And the sling went 'round and 'round
And one little stone went into the sling
And the sling went 'round and 'round

And 'round and 'round and 'round and 'round
And 'round and 'round and 'round
And one little stone went up in the air
And the giant came tumbling down

David and Jonathan

1 Samuel 18:1–4

David went to live in the king's house. There he met Jonathan, the king's son. Jonathan and David became best friends. Jonathan gave David a present. He gave David his own coat. He also gave David his sword, bow, and belt. They made a special promise to each other: "We will always be friends. We will always help each other."

God had a wonderful plan for David's life. God's blessings were on David. Soon he would become a great king and mighty soldier.

Sharing pleases God.

Jonathan showed David his friendship by sharing.

I will share with my friends.

Isn't He Wonderful

Isn't He wonderful, wonderful, wonderful
Isn't Jesus, my Lord, wonderful
Eyes have seen, ears have heard
It's recorded in God's Word
Isn't Jesus, my Lord, wonderful

David and Mephibosheth

2 Samuel 9

King Saul and his son Jonathan were both killed in battle. God chose David as the new king. In those days, the children of the old king were usually sent away. But David was a kind king. He sent for Jonathan's crippled son, Mephibosheth, to come to the palace. Mephibosheth was afraid of what David might say. But David said, "Don't be afraid. I loved Jonathan, your father. You are welcome in my house. Please come and eat dinner with me." Because of David's kindness, Mephibosheth became part of the king's family.

God said to be kind to one another.

David was kind to Mephibosheth.

I will show kindness to others.

Be Kind

To the tune of "Row, Row, Row Your Boat"

**Be kind every day
Be kind in every way.
Show the love of God above
In all you do and say!**

Elijah's Victory

1 Kings 18:1, 17–39

Bad King Ahab and his wife did not love God. They served a false god named Baal. One day the prophet Elijah spoke, "Let's find out who is the true God." They agreed to build an altar and lay wood upon it. Then Elijah said that those who served Baal should call to him and ask that fire come down from heaven onto the altar. Then Elijah would pray the same thing to God.

All day Ahab's prophets prayed to their false god Baal. Nothing happened. Then Elijah poured water all over his altar three times and called to God: "Today, Lord, let it be known that You are the one true God!" Instantly fire fell from heaven. Everyone knew Elijah's God was the one true God.

There is only one God.

Elijah told people about the one true God.

I will tell people about God.

Climb Sunshine Mountain

Climb, climb up Sunshine Mountain
Heavenly breezes blow
Climb, climb up Sunshine Mountain
Faces all aglow
Turn, turn from sin and sorrow
Look to God on high
Climb, climb up Sunshine Mountain, you and I

Elijah's Chariot of Fire

2 Kings 2:9–12

Elijah was God's messenger and served God for many years. When Elijah was old, he needed a helper. He chose Elisha. Elisha loved God too. Elijah asked Elisha if there was something he could do for him before he left. Elisha told him he wanted a double share of the spirit God had given him. Elijah said, "You have asked for a hard thing. But if you see me go into heaven, it will be yours."

Suddenly, a chariot and horses of fire appeared. Elisha saw Elijah go up into heaven in a whirlwind. Just as Elijah promised, Elisha received God's power.

God has prepared a home in heaven for those who serve Him.

Elijah was taken to heaven in a fiery chariot.

God has a home in heaven for me.

Swing Low, Sweet Chariot

Swing low, sweet chariot
Comin' for to carry me home
Swing low, sweet chariot
Comin' for to carry me home

I looked over Jordan and what did I see
Comin' for to carry me home
A band of angels comin' after me
Comin' for to carry me home

Naaman

2 Kings 5:1–14

Naaman commanded the army of Aram. He was a very important man. But he was also a very sick man. He had sores all over his body.

One day Naaman heard about a man named Elisha. Elisha had done many wonderful things. Naaman went to Elisha's house to ask him how to get well. Elisha prayed and God told him exactly what to do. Elisha told the servant to tell Naaman to go to the Jordan River and wash seven times. Six times wouldn't do. So Naaman went down into the water seven times. The sores were gone! God made Naaman well!

We should trust God and follow His instructions.

Naaman did exactly as God said, and he was healed.

I will do exactly what God says.

O Happy Day

O happy day that fixed my choice
On You, my Savior and my God
Well may this glowing heart rejoice
And tell its joyfulness abroad

Happy day, happy day
When Jesus washed my sins away
He taught me how to watch and pray
And live rejoicing every day
Happy day, happy day
When Jesus washed my sins away

Nehemiah's Wall

Nehemiah 1–2

Nehemiah was a servant of the king. One day Nehemiah's brother came from their homeland with sad news. The walls of Jerusalem, where they used to live, were falling down. This made Nehemiah very sad. Nehemiah didn't know how to get the wall rebuilt. So he did the only thing he knew to do. He prayed. He asked God to help his people.

The king noticed Nehemiah's sad face. He asked, "Why are you so sad?" Nehemiah told him about the broken-down wall. The king was kind. He said, "Go and help your people rebuild the wall. Come back when it is finished." Nehemiah thanked God for answering his prayer.

When you don't know what to do, pray.

Nehemiah prayed for help, and God helped him.

When I don't know what to do, I will pray.

Sweet Hour of Prayer

Sweet hour of prayer
Sweet hour of prayer
That calls me from a world of care
And bids me at my Father's throne
Make all my wants and wishes known

In seasons of distress and grief
My soul has often found relief
And oft escaped the tempter's snare
By Thy return, sweet hour of prayer

Queen Esther

Esther 1–10

Esther, a beautiful Jewish girl, married a king. Esther's cousin Mordecai was the king's good helper. Haman was also a helper, but he was bad. Haman didn't like the Jews. He had a plan to kill Mordecai and all the Jews.

Mordecai heard about Haman's plan and told Esther, "Perhaps God has made you queen for such a time as this." Queen Esther asked the king to save her and her people. She told the king about Haman's evil plan to kill all the Jews. The king was angry with Haman. Because of Esther, God's people were saved!

You were born at just the right time.

Esther was born at just the right time to serve God.

I was born at the right time to serve God.

For Such a Time as This!

To the tune of "Alouette"

Esther, Esther
Beautiful Queen Esther
Esther, Esther, servant of the Lord!

Born for such a time as this! (Born for such a time as this)
You served the Lord (Served the Lord)
Faithfully (Faithfully)
And saved God's people!

Job

Job was a good man and a blessing to others. God blessed him with a wonderful family, wealth, and good health. Every morning Job thanked God for his many blessings.

One day Job lost all he owned. Then Job's children were killed in a great storm. But Job still trusted God. He said, "The Lord gives, and the Lord takes away. Praise the name of the Lord!" Then Job became very sick. Job did not blame God for his sickness. Job knew there are some things we cannot understand. God was pleased with Job and healed him. And He gave Job more children, crops, and animals!

We should praise the Lord in good times and bad. Job praised the Lord, even in bad times.

I will praise the Lord all the time!

God Is So Good

God is so good, God is so good
God is so good, He's so good to me

He answers prayer, He answers prayer
He answers prayer, He's so good to me

He cares for me, He cares for me
He cares for me, He's so good to me

I love Him so, I love Him so
I love Him so, He's so good to me

Ezekiel's Wheel

Ezekiel 1

The prophet Ezekiel had a dream as he looked up into the sky. He saw a stormy wind with lightning flashes and very bright lights. He saw four angels with wings. Beside each angel was a sparkling wheel. Each wheel had a smaller wheel spinning inside it. Above the angels was a beautiful throne, and on the throne was a figure like a man. A brilliant light like a rainbow surrounded the man.

Ezekiel's dream was about God. How mighty our God is! He is both powerful and wonderful. Ezekiel bowed down to show God honor and respect.

God is greater than we are.

Ezekiel bowed down to honor God.

I will honor and respect God.

Ezekiel's Wheel

Ezekiel saw a wheel
Way up in the middle of the air
A wheel within a wheel
Way in the middle of the air
The little wheel turned by faith
And the big wheel turned by the grace of God
Ezekiel saw a wheel
Way up in the middle of the air

Ezekiel's Dry Bones

Ezekiel 37:1–14

One night Ezekiel had another strange dream. He dreamed he was taken to the middle of a large valley full of old, dry bones. God asked, "Can these bones live?"

Ezekiel answered, "I don't know, Lord. Only You know that!" Ezekiel watched as the dry bones stood up, were covered in muscles and skin, were given new breath, and became an army.

Then God explained the dream. "My people are sad. They think things will not get better. Tell them that things will get better. They will return to the Promised Land."

Ezekiel told the people what God said. "Dry bones can live. All things are possible with God!"

All things are possible with God.

Ezekiel believed that God could do anything.

I believe God can do all things!

Dry Bones

To the tune of "Dem Bones"

Dem bones, dem bones, dem dry bones
Dem bones, dem bones, dem dry bones
Dem bones, dem bones, dem dry bones
Now hear the word of the Lord

Oh, Ezekiel connected dem dry bones
Oh, Ezekiel connected dem dry bones
Oh, Ezekiel connected dem dry bones
Now hear the word of the Lord

Shadrach, Meshach, and Abednego

Daniel 3

A bad king made a golden statue. He made everyone bow down before the statue when the music played. "If you don't bow down," he said, "I will throw you into the fire." Everyone bowed except Shadrach, Meshach, and Abednego. They would not bow down to a statue. They would only bow down to God. So the king had the men thrown into the hot fire.

But then the king saw something that amazed him. "Didn't I throw three men into the fire?" he said. "I see four men walking around!" He called Shadrach, Meshach, and Abednego to come out of the fire. They were not even burned! Then the king believed in God and praised Him.

When we are afraid, we can trust in God.

Shadrach, Meshach, and Abednego trusted God, even when they were afraid.

I will trust God, even when I am afraid.

His Banner over Me Is Love

The Lord is mine and I am His
His banner over me is love
The Lord is mine and I am His
His banner over me is love
The Lord is mine and I am His
His banner over me is love
His banner over me is love

Daniel in the Lions' Den

Daniel 6

Daniel loved God and prayed to Him every day. The king planned to put Daniel in charge of the whole kingdom. This made the other leaders jealous. They wanted to get rid of Daniel. So they came up with an evil plan. They made a law that said it was wrong to pray to anyone but the king. But Daniel was a good man. He kept praying to God.

The bad men took Daniel to the king. "Daniel broke the law! Throw him to the lions!" Daniel was dropped into a pit full of hungry lions. But God sent an angel to shut the lions' mouths. God saved Daniel.

God answers our prayers
when we are in trouble.

Daniel prayed when he needed help.

I will pray when I need help.

Whisper a Prayer

Whisper a prayer in the morning
Whisper a prayer at noon
Whisper a prayer in the evening
To keep your heart in tune

God answers prayer in the morning
God answers prayer at noon
God answers prayer in the evening
So keep your heart in tune

Jonah Runs Away from God

Jonah 1:1–15

God told Jonah to go to Nineveh and tell the people there about God's love. Jonah didn't want to go. He tried to run away from God on a ship. But he couldn't hide from God.

God caused a big storm. The sailors were afraid, but Jonah was fast asleep. They woke Jonah. "Pray to your God. Ask Him to save us."

Jonah knew the storm was his fault. Then Jonah said a strange thing: "Throw me overboard, and the storm will stop."

They threw Jonah into the water, and down he sank. Then the sea became calm again.

God has a job for everyone.

God had a job for Jonah.

I will do the job that God has for me.

I Will Call Upon the Lord

I will call upon the Lord (I will call upon the Lord)
Who is worthy to be praised (Who is worthy to be praised)
So shall I be saved from my enemies (So shall I be saved from my enemies)

The Lord liveth, and blessed be the Rock!
And let the God of my salvation be exalted!
The Lord liveth, and blessed be the Rock!
And let the God of my salvation be exalted!

Jonah and the Big Fish

Jonah 1:17–3:10

As Jonah sank beneath the waves, he was swallowed by a big fish. Jonah was in the stomach of that fish for three days and three nights! He was sorry he had disobeyed. He prayed and prayed. He asked God to forgive him for running away.

God's love is so wonderful. God forgave Jonah. So God told the big fish to spit Jonah up on the seashore. Then Jonah obeyed God. He got up and went to Nineveh. He told the people to stop doing bad things. The people told God they were sorry. And God saved the people of Nineveh!

God is a forgiving God.

He forgave Jonah even though he disobeyed.

I know God will forgive me if I say I'm sorry.

Who Did Swallow Jonah?

Who did, who did, who did, who did
Who did swallow Jo, Jo, Jo, Jo
Who did swallow Jonah, who did swallow Jonah
Who did swallow Jonah down?

Whale did, whale did, whale did, whale did
Whale did swallow Jo, Jo, Jo, Jo
Whale did swallow Jonah, whale did swallow Jonah
Whale did swallow Jonah down

David's Shepherd

Psalm 23

When you have to make a big decision, who helps you? When you don't know which way to go, who gives you directions? When you need protection from life's many dangers, where do you go?

When David needed help, he went to his Good Shepherd. Who is that, you ask? "The Lord is my Shepherd," David wrote. "He leads me. He protects me. He restores me. He comforts me when I'm afraid, and He gives me everything I need. God's goodness will always be with me!" And like a sheep, David followed Him.

We can trust God to lead and protect us.

David followed God like sheep follow a shepherd.

I will follow God and know He'll protect me.

Psalm 23

To the tune of "Joyful, Joyful, We Adore Thee"

Know the Lord, He is my shepherd
And I shall not want at all
Yes, the Lord, He is my shepherd
And I shall not want at all

He makes me lie down in green pastures
He leads me beside still waters pure
He restores my soul and guides me
With His love I am secure

David's Fear

Psalm 56

David was very brave. He had marched down into the valley to fight a giant named Goliath. He had led great armies into battle and won the victory. But in Psalm 56 we see another side of David. We see David alone and afraid. His enemies were chasing him, calling him names, and doing bad things.

David's eyes were full of tears as he cried out to God, "When I am afraid, I will trust in You." David knew that God could help him. God is bigger than any fear!

God can calm our biggest fears.

David trusted God when he was afraid.

I will trust God to help me when I'm afraid.

When I Am Afraid

To the tune of "Skinnamarink"

Oh, when I am afraid, my Lord
Oh, when I am afraid
I'll trust in You!
Oh, when I am afraid, my Lord
Oh, when I am afraid
I'll trust in You!

Whether in the morning
Or in the afternoon.
If I am in trouble
I will call on you!

David Praises the Lord

Psalm 71; 148; 150

David wrote many songs in the book of Psalms. He knew it was good to praise the Lord. When we praise the Lord, we tell Him how good and wonderful we think He is. When we praise God, we let Him know how much we love Him.

David praised the Lord with the harp. He praised Him with singing and dancing. He praised Him first thing in the morning. Then he praised Him in the evening when the sun went down. And do you know what? We can too!

It is good to praise the Lord!

David praised the Lord all the time.

I will praise the Lord and tell Him I love Him.

Praise the Lord Together

Praise the Lord together singing
Alleluia, alleluia, alleluia
Praise the Lord together singing
Alleluia, alleluia, alleluia

God's Great Big World

Psalm 136

When David was a shepherd boy, he spent many nights alone. On the hillside it was quiet, so David wrote a lot of songs.

In Psalm 136, David wrote that God made the heavens. He made every star that shines. God made the earth. He made everything that lives on earth. And God made the skies and the sea.

God shows His love for us in nature around us. Whenever we see a tree, a mountain, the ocean, or anything else in nature, we can thank God for His amazing creation. This truly is our Father's world.

Praise God because He made our world.

David praised God for making the heavens and the earth.

I see all God made, and I praise Him.

This Is My Father's World

This is my Father's world and to my listening ears
All nature sings and 'round me rings the music of the spheres
This is my Father's world, I rest me in the thought
Of rocks and trees, of skies and seas
His hand the wonders wrought

This is my Father's world, the birds their carols raise
The morning light, the lily white, declare their Maker's praise
This is my Father's world, He shines in all that's fair
In rustling grass I hear Him pass
He speaks to me everywhere

As Wise As an Owl

Proverbs 23:12

You've heard the saying "as wise as an owl." Do you know who was the wisest man who ever lived? The Bible says there was no one wiser than Solomon.

What were some of the things this wise man did? First, he knew God's Word. Then he applied God's Word to his life. To "apply" means to put into practice. Solomon learned the importance of giving to others, and he gave generously. He also learned to help others, and he helped many people in the kingdom.

How can you be wise like Solomon? Know God's Word, and apply what the Bible says. Then you'll be as wise as an owl too!

It is wise to put God's Word into practice.

Solomon was wise to apply God's Word.

I will read my Bible and do what it teaches.

All Creatures of Our God and King

All creatures of our God and King
Lift up your voice and with us sing
Alleluia, alleluia
Thou burning sun with golden beam
Thou silver moon with softer gleam

O praise Him, O praise Him
Alleluia, alleluia, alleluia

Gabriel Visits Mary

Luke 1:26–38

A young woman named Mary loved God with all her heart. One day an angel named Gabriel came to visit Mary. He had a message from God. When Mary saw the angel, she was afraid. But the angel said, "Do not be afraid. God is pleased with you. He is going to give you a special baby. The baby will be God's own Son. You will name Him Jesus."

Mary was amazed. She asked the angel, "How can this be true?"

The angel answered, "Nothing is impossible with God!" Mary believed and thanked God.

Nothing is impossible with God.

Mary believed God could do anything.

I believe God can do anything too!

Fairest Lord Jesus

Fairest Lord Jesus, ruler of all nature
O Thou of God and man the Son
Thee will I cherish, Thee will I honor
Thou my soul's glory, joy, and crown

Fair is the sunshine, fairer still the moonlight
And all the twinkling starry host
Jesus shines brighter, Jesus shines purer
Than all the angels heaven can boast

97

The Savior Is Born

Luke 2:1–14

Mary and Joseph traveled from Nazareth to Bethlehem. "Joseph," she said, "it's time for my baby to be born!"

Joseph looked for a place to stay. But everywhere he stopped the inn owners gave the same answer: "We have no room." Joseph found a stable full of cows and sheep. Mary and Joseph could stay there.

On that special night the baby Jesus was born. Mary wrapped Jesus in cloth and laid Him in a manger, a feeding box full of hay. The animals must have been very surprised! That night angels sang and praised God: "Glory to God in the highest, and peace on earth!" Jesus, God's Son, was born!

God always takes care of our needs.

He gave baby Jesus a bed.

I will trust God to take care of me.

Away in a Manger

Away in manger, no crib for a bed
The little Lord Jesus laid down His sweet head
The stars in the sky look down where He lay
The little Lord Jesus asleep on the hay

The cattle are lowing, the baby awakes
But little Lord Jesus no crying He makes
I love Thee, Lord Jesus, look down from the sky
And stay by my cradle 'til morning is nigh

Wise Men Come

Matthew 2:1–12

The three wise men had seen a lot of stars. But they had never seen a special star like this one! This star was moving across the eastern sky. And night after night they followed it. They knew God was using it to guide them to a new king.

The journey was long. But finally the star stopped and came to rest over the little town of Bethlehem. Beneath the star they found baby Jesus. When they saw Him, they bowed down and worshipped Him. They gave Jesus gifts of gold, frankincense, and myrrh. They knew Jesus was Lord.

God guides us to Jesus so we can worship Him.

Wise men followed the star to worship Jesus.

I will worship Jesus.

We Three Kings

We three kings of Orient are
Bearing gifts we traverse afar
Field and fountain, moor and mountain
Following yonder star

Oh, star of wonder, star of night
Star with royal beauty bright
Westward leading, still proceeding
Guide us to Thy perfect light

Jesus in the Temple

Luke 2:41–52

When Jesus was twelve years old, Mary and Joseph took Him to a feast in Jerusalem. They walked for several days to get there. It was fun traveling with their friends.

On the way home, Mary and Joseph realized Jesus wasn't with them. They couldn't find Him among their family or friends. They hurried back to Jerusalem. They looked for three days! Finally they found Jesus in the temple. Mary said, "Jesus, where have you been?"

Jesus said, "Didn't you know I'd be in My Father's house?" Jesus loved to go to God's house and talk about God.

It is good to learn about God.

Jesus loved to go to the temple and talk about God.

I like to learn about God too.

Jesus in the Morning

Jesus, Jesus
Jesus in the morning
Jesus at the noontide
Jesus, Jesus
Jesus when the sun goes down

Praise Him, praise Him
Praise Him in the morning
Praise Him at the noontide
Praise Him, praise Him
Praise Him when the sun goes down

John Baptizes Jesus

Matthew 3:13–17; Mark 1:9–11;
Luke 3:21–22; John 1:29–34

John the Baptist lived in the desert. He ate wild honey and locusts. John told people about God. Jesus said that John was a great man.

One day while John was baptizing believers, Jesus came to him. He walked up to John and said, "Baptize Me."

John knew Jesus was God's Son. He said, "I should be baptized by You!"

But John did as Jesus asked. Down into the water Jesus went. When He came up, the Spirit of God came and landed on His shoulder. It looked like a dove. God said, "This is My Son, and I love Him."

Baptism shows the world that we love Jesus.

Jesus was baptized and pleased God.

When I am baptized, God will be pleased.

Down by the Riverside

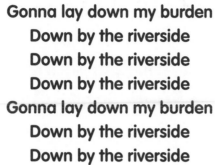

Gonna lay down my burden
Down by the riverside
Down by the riverside
Down by the riverside
Gonna lay down my burden
Down by the riverside
Down by the riverside

Jesus Calls His Disciples

Matthew 4:18–22; Mark 1:16–20; Luke 5:1–11; John 1:35–42

Jesus needed some helpers. One day Jesus was walking beside the Sea of Galilee. He saw some fishermen working. Peter and Andrew were in a boat fishing. James and John were in another boat mending their nets. Jesus called to them, "Come and follow Me. I will make you fishers of men." At once, they left their boats to follow Jesus. They were the first disciples. They would tell others about Him.

Jesus calls us to be His disciples.

The disciples left their nets and followed Jesus.

I will follow Jesus and tell others about Him.

I Have Decided to Follow Jesus

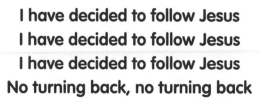

I have decided to follow Jesus
I have decided to follow Jesus
I have decided to follow Jesus
No turning back, no turning back

In everything, child, give thanks and praise Him
In everything, child, give thanks and praise Him
In everything, child, give thanks and praise Him
No turning back, no turning back

The Beatitudes

Matthew 5:1–12; Luke 6:20–26

Many people came to hear Jesus teach. One day the crowd was so big Jesus had to go up on a mountainside. When He got there, He told everyone about the Beatitudes.

He said, "People who are sad now will be happy. And people who are kind will be shown kindness. The pure will see God. God will satisfy those who want to know Him more. And those who are treated badly because they do good things will be joyful. Be glad. We have great rewards waiting in heaven!"

Following Jesus makes us happy.

Many people follow Jesus.

I will follow Jesus too.

Amazing Grace

Amazing grace, how sweet the sound
That saved a wretch like me
I once was lost, but now I'm found
Was blind, but now I see

When we've been there ten thousand years
Bright shining as the sun
We've no less days to sing God's praise
Than when we'd first begun

Shine for Jesus

Matthew 5:14–16

Every morning the bright yellow sun comes up. As the sun begins to shine, darkness goes away. Jesus said that we should be like sunbeams. We are to bring God's light to a dark world.

When we are kind, we bring light to the world. When we tell our friends about God's love, we bring light to the world. When we do good things that honor God, other people will want to praise God too. Yes, Jesus wants us to shine, just like a sunbeam!

Jesus' followers do good things to honor Him.

Jesus said we are a light to the world when we do good things that honor Him.

I will shine for Jesus.

I'll Be a Sunbeam

Jesus wants me for a sunbeam
To shine for Him each day
In every way try to please Him
At home, at school, at play

A sunbeam, a sunbeam
Jesus wants me for a sunbeam
A sunbeam, a sunbeam
I'll be a sunbeam for Him

Pray Like Jesus

Matthew 6:5–13; Mark 1:35; Luke 11:2–4

Praying is talking with God. Jesus prayed every day. He taught His followers how to pray. He was a good example. Jesus said we should find a quiet place where we can be alone with God. Early in the morning, while it was still dark, Jesus got up. He left the house and went to a place to be alone with God. There He talked to His heavenly Father. Jesus also talked to His heavenly Father in the morning, afternoon, evening— all the time! We can talk to God too, just like Jesus.

Talk with God.

Jesus showed us how to pray.

I can pray anytime.

I've Got the Joy, Joy, Joy, Joy

I've got the joy, joy, joy, joy
Down in my heart (Where?)
Down in my heart (Where?)
Down in my heart
I've got the joy, joy, joy, joy
Down in my heart (Where?)
Down in my heart to stay

Do Not Judge

Matthew 7:1–5; Luke 6:37–42

Jesus doesn't want us to judge another person's actions. When we judge, we decide if someone is doing good or bad. That's not our job; it's God's job. God wants us to make right choices and look at our own lives.

Jesus said, "Do not judge others. If you do, you will be judged. In the same way you judge others, you will be judged." If we're harsh and unkind, we will be judged the very same way. Before we tell others about something they are doing wrong, we must stop doing wrong ourselves.

We should not judge others.

Jesus said, "Do not judge."

I will not judge what others do.

I Am Bound for the Promised Land

On Jordan's stormy banks I stand
And cast a wishful eye
To Canaan's fair and happy land
Where my possessions lie

I am bound for the Promised Land
I am bound for the Promised Land
O who will come and go with me
I am bound for the Promised Land

Ask, Seek, and Knock

Matthew 7:7–8; Luke 11:9–10

Jesus taught His disciples that they should never stop praying. He said, "Keep asking in prayer, and it will be given to you. Keep seeking, and you will find what you are looking for. Keep knocking, and the door will be opened to you!"

God always hears our prayers, and He will answer! God wants to talk to you, and He's glad when you talk to Him and ask for your needs. So never quit praying!

God has promised to answer our prayers.

Jesus said to ask God for what you need.

I know God hears and answers my prayers.

Ask, Seek, and Knock

To the tune of "I'm a Little Teapot"

Friend, we have a promise
Yes, we do
Ask and it shall be given to you
Read it in the Bible
Yes, it's true!
Just ask and it will be given to you!

The Golden Rule

Matthew 7:12; Luke 6:31

Jesus taught His twelve disciples a very important lesson. He said we should always treat others the way we want to be treated. It's called the golden rule. It's golden because it's the most valuable lesson we can ever learn. It's called a rule because we need to do this all the time, not just some of the time.

If you want to be treated kindly, treat others with kindness. If you want to be loved, show love to others. If we obey this rule, we will be happy, and God will be pleased.

Show kindness to everyone.

Jesus said to treat other people the way you want to be treated.

I will show kindness and obey the golden rule.

The Golden Rule

To the tune of "If You're Happy and You Know It"

Do to others as you'd have them do to you (clap, clap)
Do to others as you'd have them do to you (clap, clap)
Sister, brother, father, mother
Oh, be kind to one another
Do to others as you'd have them do to you!

The Wise Man Built His House

Matthew 7:24–29; Luke 6:47–49

Jesus said there are wise people and foolish people. He said a wise person is like a builder who builds his house upon a rock. Rocks are strong and do not wash away. So a house built on a rock will stand.

The Bible is like a solid rock. It's God's Word to us. It tells us about the best way to live. If we do the things the Bible says to do, we will be strong. Wise people read the Bible and do what it says. When we build our lives on the solid rock of God's Word, we will stand strong for Jesus!

Wise people do what the Bible says.

Jesus taught about wise and foolish people.

I will do what the Bible says.

The Wise Man Built His House Upon the Rock

The wise man built his house upon the rock
The wise man built his house upon the rock
The wise man built his house upon the rock
And the rains came tumbling down

The rains came down and the floods came up
The rains came down and the floods came up
The rains came down and the floods came up
And the house on the rock stood firm

A Hole in the Roof

Matthew 9:1–8; Mark 2:1–12; Luke 5:17–25

Jesus was teaching inside a house full of people. There were even people standing outside, looking through the windows and doors! Four men arrived. They were carrying their friend, who could not walk. They wanted Jesus to heal him.

When they couldn't get through the crowd, they had an idea. They carried their friend on his mat up onto the roof. They made a hole in the roof and lowered their friend down. Jesus told the man to pick up his mat and go home. The man stood up! His friends were glad, and all the people praised God!

Jesus can help our friends.

Four men brought their friend to Jesus.

I will bring my friends to Jesus.

Kumbaya

Kumbaya, my Lord, kumbaya
Kumbaya, my Lord, kumbaya
Kumbaya, my Lord, kumbaya
Oh, Lord, kumbaya

Someone's singing, Lord, kumbaya
Someone's singing, Lord, kumbaya
Someone's singing, Lord, kumbaya
Oh, Lord, kumbaya

Jesus Calms the Storm

Matthew 8:23–27; Mark 4:35–41; Luke 8:22–25

One day Jesus and His disciples were sailing across a lake. He was very tired from teaching all day. So a sleepy Jesus took a nap in the back of the boat.

While He was sleeping, there came a terrible storm. The waves crashed against the boat. The disciples woke Jesus up saying, "Teacher, don't you care if we drown?"

Jesus got up, faced the wind, and shouted to the storm, "Quiet! Be still!" At His word, the wind stopped and the waters were calmed.

The disciples were amazed. They said, "Even the wind and waves obey Him!"

God is in control.

Jesus controls the wind and the sea.

I won't be afraid. God is in control.

What a Mighty Hand

To the tune of "It Takes a Worried Man to Sing a Worried Song"

Oh, what a mighty hand, a mighty hand has He
Oh, what a mighty hand, a mighty hand has He
Oh, what a mighty hand, a mighty hand has He
He calms the sea, yes, He calms the sea!

Even the wind and waves obey the voice of God
Even the wind and waves obey the voice of God
Even the wind and waves obey the voice of God
He calms the sea, yes, He calms the sea!

Jesus Heals

Matthew 9:20–22; Mark 5:25–34; Luke 8:43–48

Everywhere Jesus went there were crowds of people. Some people came to hear Him teach. Some needed His help. One woman in the crowd wanted Jesus to make her well. She thought, "If I could just get close enough to touch His clothes, I'm sure I would get well!"

She pushed through the crowd until she got close to Jesus. She stretched out her hand and touched the edge of His coat. As soon as she touched Him, she was well!

Jesus asked, "Who touched Me?" The woman then thanked Jesus for making her well.

Jesus has the power to heal.

He made a sick woman well.

When I am sick, I will ask Jesus to help me.

What a Friend We Have in Jesus

What a friend we have in Jesus
All our sins and griefs to bear
What a privilege to carry
Everything to God in prayer

O what peace we often forfeit
O what needless pain we bear
All because we do not carry
Everything to God in prayer

Parable of the Pearl

Matthew 13:45–46

Jesus said the kingdom of heaven is like a pearl. Once a man found a pearl worth lots of money. It was the most beautiful pearl in all the world. To get it, he would have to sell everything he had. But it was worth it!

Heaven is like that. There is no treasure on earth that compares to heaven. It is better than anything in this world. It is worth everything you have to get it. Earthly things don't last long, but heaven is forever!

Heaven is more wonderful than anything on earth.

We should let nothing on earth keep us from heaven.

I will thank God for making heaven for me!

Happy All the Time

I'm in right, outright, upright, downright
Happy all the time
I'm in right, outright, upright, downright
Happy all the time
Since Jesus Christ came in
And cleansed my heart from sin
I'm in right, outright, upright, downright
Happy all the time

Parable of the Net

Matthew 13:47–50

Once Jesus told a story about a fisherman. This fisherman threw his net out into the lake. Many fish swam into the net. The fisherman waited until the net was full. Then he pulled the net in. He began to sort the good fish from the bad fish.

Jesus explained, "Heaven is like the fisherman's net. Everyone wants to go to heaven. But one day the angels will sort out the people who really love God from the people who don't. The people who really love God will go to heaven. But those who do not love God will not."

All Christians will go to heaven.

Heaven is a wonderful place.

I love God. I will go to heaven!

I Will Make You Fishers of Men

I will make you fishers of men
Fishers of men, fishers of men
I will make you fishers of men
If you follow me

If you follow me, if you follow me
I will make you fishers of men
If you follow me

Jesus Loves You!

John 3:16

In the Bible, we find a wonderful promise. John 3:16 says that God loves you and me. He loves your mom and dad. He loves everyone in your family. He loves all your neighbors. In fact, He loves everyone in your city and state. Yes, His love is so big that it reaches out to everyone in the whole world.

God did something to prove that He loves us. He gave His only Son, Jesus, to save everyone who believes in Him. Now all these people can live in heaven forever if they trust Jesus to be their Savior. What a wonderful promise!

God loved us so much that He sent His Son!

Jesus came to save us.

I thank God for sending Jesus!

For God So Loved the World

To the tune of "The Wheels on the Bus"

**For God above so loved the world
Loved the world, loved the world
For God above so loved the world
Praise His name forever!**

He gave His one and only Son
Only Son, only Son.
He gave His one and only Son
Praise His Name forever!

Pool at Bethesda

John 5:1–9

Bethesda was a very special pool. Every day sick and hurting people went there. The water of Bethesda was usually calm. But sometimes an angel would come and stir the water. When the water stirred, the first person into the pool would be healed.

One day Jesus saw a man who couldn't walk sitting by the pool. Jesus asked him, "Do you want to get well?"

The man said, "Yes, but I have no one to help me get into the pool."

Then Jesus said, "Pick up your mat and walk." The man obeyed and was healed. He stood up and walked away happy!

Jesus has the power to heal.

He healed the crippled man.

I know Jesus can make sick people well.

Rolled Away, Rolled Away

Rolled away, rolled away, rolled away
All the burdens of my heart rolled away
Rolled away, rolled away, rolled away
All the burdens of my heart rolled away
All the sin had to go
'Neath the crimson flow, hallelujah!
Rolled away, rolled away, rolled away
All the burdens of my heart rolled away

Feeding of 5,000

Matthew 14:13–21; Mark 6:35–44; Luke 9:11–17; John 6:1–14

People came from near and far to hear Jesus teach. One day many people gathered to listen. After a while the people were hungry. Jesus asked His disciples to feed them. They said, "We don't have enough money to feed them, but here is a boy who has five loaves of bread and two fish. He is willing to share."

Jesus took the boy's lunch, looked up to heaven, and gave thanks. He began breaking the bread and fish into pieces. It fed more than five thousand people, and there were twelve basketfuls left! A little bit goes a long way in Jesus' hands.

Give what you have to Jesus, and He will bless it.

A little boy shared his lunch with a crowd.

I will share what I have.

Get on Board, Little Children

The gospel train is comin'
The wheels go 'round and 'round
Everyone is happy
This train is heaven bound

Get on board, little children
Get on board, little children
Get on board, little children
There's room for many a-more

Jesus Walks on Water

Matthew 14:22–32; Mark 6:45–51; John 6:16–21

One evening the disciples were rowing their boat across the lake. Suddenly, a mighty wind blew. It caused their boat to be tossed back and forth on the waves. Jesus saw they were in trouble. He went out to them, walking on water!

When the disciples saw Jesus walking on the lake, they thought He was a ghost. They were afraid. Jesus called to them, "Don't be afraid!" As He climbed into the boat, the wind calmed down.

The disciples were amazed. They said, "Truly You are the Son of God!"

Jesus can do anything.

He even walked on water.

I am not afraid. Jesus can do anything.

He'll Be Walking Across the Water

To the tune of "She'll Be Coming 'Round the Mountain"

He'll be walking across the water when He comes
He'll be walking across the water when He comes
He'll be walking across the water, walking across the water
He'll be walking across the water when He comes

Jesus called to them, "My friends, don't be afraid!"
Jesus called to them, "My friends, don't be afraid!"
Jesus called out in the thunder, He called out in the thunder
Jesus called to them, "My friends, don't be afraid!"

Faith Is Like a Mustard Seed

Matthew 17:20; Luke 17:6

A giant oak tree wasn't always so big. It started out as a little seed. Big things usually start out small. Jesus once explained that faith in God works that way.

When we start loving God, we love just a little. But as we grow, God helps us love more and more. Our faith grows more and more, just as a seed grows into a big tree. Jesus said that if we have faith the size of a tiny mustard seed, we will be able to move mountains. As our faith grows, nothing will be impossible for us!

Faith starts small and grows big.

Faith the size of a mustard seed can move mountains.

I believe that my faith will grow and grow!

Mustard Seed Faith

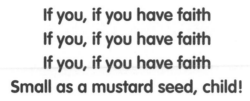

To the tune of "Skip to My Lou"

If you, if you have faith
If you, if you have faith
If you, if you have faith
Small as a mustard seed, child!

Nothing, nothing will be
Nothing, nothing will be
Nothing, nothing will be
Impossible for you, child!

Fishing for Gold

Matthew 17:24–27

Peter was worried. Jesus didn't have any money to pay the tax collector. Peter didn't have any money either. But Jesus wasn't worried. He knew God would take care of them.

Jesus told Peter to go fishing. When he caught his first fish, he was to look in the fish's mouth. Peter didn't understand, but he did as Jesus said. When Peter caught his first fish, he looked in the fish's mouth. There he found a gold coin! Now there was plenty of money to pay the taxes. God had given them what they needed.

God will take care of our needs.

He met the disciple's needs.

I will trust God to take care of me.

Children, Go Where I Send Thee

Children, go where I send thee
How shall I send thee?
I'm gonna send thee three by three
Three for the Hebrew children
Two for Paul and Silas
One for the little bitty baby
Born, born, born in Bethlehem

Throw the First Stone

John 8:1–11

The Bible says that one day Jesus was teaching the people in the temple. A woman was brought before Him. She had done a very bad thing. The people were going to throw stones at her. They asked Jesus what they should do.

Jesus wanted to show the people how to love one another. He said, "If you've never done anything wrong, throw the first stone." One by one, people started to leave. Eventually everyone had left! Jesus forgave the woman for doing wrong, and He showed the people how to love.

We should love one another.

Jesus loved and cared for sinners.

Jesus loves me, and I will love others.

Jesus Loves Me

Jesus loves me, this I know
For the Bible tells me so
Little ones to Him belong
They are weak, but He is strong

Yes, Jesus loves me
Yes, Jesus loves me
Yes, Jesus loves me
The Bible tells me so

Jesus loves me, He who died
Heaven's gate to open wide
He will wash away my sin
Let His little child come in

A Blind Man Sees

John 9:1–7

Once there was a man who was born blind. He could not see the blue sky or the sunshine. He could not see the faces of people who loved him. Jesus wanted to help this man. He did something strange. Jesus spit on the ground and made some mud. He put the mud on the blind man's eyes. Then Jesus told him to go and wash.

The blind man obeyed. And as the mud washed from his eyes, he saw the blue sky. He saw the sunshine. He was blind, but now he could see!

Jesus has the power to heal.

He healed a blind man.

I will praise Jesus for His healing power.

Rejoice in the Lord Always

Rejoice in the Lord always
And again I say, rejoice
Rejoice in the Lord always
And again I say, rejoice
Rejoice, rejoice
And again I say, rejoice
Rejoice, rejoice
And again I say, rejoice

Jesus, the Good Shepherd

John 10:11–14

Jesus once said that people are like sheep and He is like a good shepherd. Sheep can get lost easily and don't always know which way to go. That's why they must listen for the shepherd's voice. They must follow him. Sheep never follow a stranger's voice. In fact, they run away from strangers.

Jesus said, "I am the Good Shepherd, and I am ready to protect My sheep." Jesus loves you and will take care of you!

Jesus is the Good Shepherd.

He loves and protects His sheep.

I know Jesus loves me
and will take care of me.

I Am the Good Shepherd

To the tune of "On Top of Old Smoky"

I am the Good Shepherd
The One from above
My life I lay down for
The sheep that I love!
I am the Good Shepherd
So don't ever fear
For like a Good Shepherd
I'll always be near!

The Good Samaritan

Luke 10:25–37

A teacher of the law asked Jesus, "You said we are to love our neighbor as ourselves. Who is our neighbor?"

Jesus answered with a story. "A man was traveling to Jericho. Robbers beat him and took everything. A priest came along, but he passed by on the other side of the road. A temple worker also passed by without stopping to help. But a man from Samaria saw the hurt man. He stopped and helped him!"

Then Jesus said, "Which one was a good neighbor?"

The teacher answered, "The one who treated him kindly."

Jesus said, "Go and do the same thing!"

We are to love our neighbors as ourselves.

Jesus says that we should be like the good Samaritan.

I will be a good neighbor and help others.

Be a Good Samaritan

To the tune of "Polly Wolly Doodle"

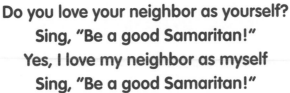

Do you love your neighbor as yourself?
Sing, "Be a good Samaritan!"
Yes, I love my neighbor as myself
Sing, "Be a good Samaritan!"

Fare thee well, fare thee well
Fare thee well, dear child of faith!
Come share the love of Jesus,
Sing to everyone who sees us,
"Be a good Samaritan!"

151

The Lost Sheep

Matthew 18:12–14; Luke 15:4–7

Jesus told His disciples a story. He wanted to teach them that God wants everyone to go to heaven. "If you had a hundred sheep and one was lost, what would you do? Wouldn't you leave the ninety-nine sheep in the meadow and look until you found the lost one? And when you found him, what would you do? Wouldn't you call your friends and say, 'Let's be happy, for I have found my lost sheep!'" Jesus said, "In the very same way, there is much happiness in heaven when one lost sinner comes to the Lord."

Lost people need to know about Jesus.

Jesus wants everyone to believe in Him.

I will tell people about Jesus.

Everybody Ought to Know

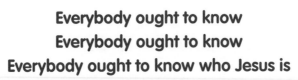

Everybody ought to know
Everybody ought to know
Everybody ought to know who Jesus is

He's the lily of the valley
He's the bright and morning star
He's the fairest of ten thousand
Everybody ought to know

Everybody ought to know
Everybody ought to know
Everybody ought to know who Jesus is

The Prodigal Son

Luke 15:11–32

Jesus told this story: "A man had two sons. One day the younger son took his money and traveled to a faraway land. There he wasted all his money. So he took a job feeding pigs. At times, he was so hungry he even thought about eating some of the pigs' food. Then he thought, *If I go home and say I'm sorry, maybe my father will let me work for food.* He traveled back to his father's house. While the boy was still far from the house, his father saw him. He ran to meet him, saying, 'My son is home!' And he hugged and kissed his son."

Jesus' story teaches us that God is our loving, forgiving Father.

God forgives us when we ask Him.

The father forgave his son.

If I make bad choices, I will come back to my forgiving God.

I Will Sing of the Mercies of the Lord

I will sing of the mercies of the Lord forever
I will sing, I will sing
I will sing of the mercies of the Lord forever
I will sing of the mercies of the Lord

With my mouth will I make known
Thy faithfulness, thy faithfulness
With my mouth will I make known
Thy faithfulness to all generations

Lazarus Lives

John 11:1–44

Aman named Lazarus was very sick. As he grew worse and worse, his family feared he might die. His sisters Mary and Martha sent a message to Jesus: "Come quickly! Our brother, Lazarus, is very sick." But Jesus waited two days.

When Jesus finally got there, Martha said, "Why didn't you come more quickly? Lazarus has died!"

Jesus walked to the tomb where Lazarus lay. He shouted, "Lazarus, come out!" Suddenly Lazarus walked out of the tomb. Jesus had performed a miracle! God's timing was perfect. Lazarus was alive again!

God helps us at just the right time.

Lazarus lived again.

I will wait on Jesus.
His timing is right for me.

Father, We Thank Thee

Father, we thank Thee for the night
And for the pleasant morning light
For rest and food and loving care
And all that makes the world so fair

Help us to do the things we should
To be to others kind and good
In all we do, in all we say
To grow more loving every day

Ten Sick Men

Luke 17:11–19

As Jesus was traveling, he saw ten sick men who had a terrible disease called leprosy. The men called to Him, "Jesus, help us! Please make us well."

What Jesus said next was very strange. He said, "Go and show yourselves to the priests." They were still sick, but because the ten men believed, they started walking toward the temple.

As they went, the men began to feel better. With every step, they felt better and better. They were being healed. But only one man came back to thank Jesus. It is good to say thank you to Jesus!

It's good to give thanks to the Lord.

One healed man gave thanks to Jesus.

I will remember to say, "Thank You, Jesus."

Come Bless the Lord

Come bless the Lord (Come bless the Lord)
All ye servants of the Lord (All ye servants of the Lord)
Who stand by night (Who stand by night)
In the house of the Lord (In the house of the Lord)
Lift up your hands (Lift up your hands)
In the holy place (In the holy place)
And bless the Lord (And bless the Lord)
And bless the Lord (And bless the Lord)

Jesus Loves Children

Matthew 19:13–14; Mark 10:13–16; Luke 18:15–17

The boys and girls were so happy. They were going to meet Jesus! But when they came to the place where Jesus was teaching, His disciples stopped them. They said, "Jesus is an important man. He is too busy for children. Go away!"

Then Jesus said, "Let the children come to Me." He sat them on His lap, hugged them, and blessed them. Yes, Jesus loves the little children. He loves all the children of the world!

Jesus loves all children.

The children came to Jesus.

I will come to Jesus because He loves me.

Jesus Loves the Little Children

Jesus loves the little children
All the children of the world
Every nation, everywhere
They are surely in His care
Jesus loves the little children of the world

Zacchaeus

Luke 19:1–10

Jesus was coming to town. All the people wanted to see him. But Zacchaeus was not tall enough to see over the crowds. *How will I ever see Jesus?* he thought. *The crowds are tall, and I'm so short!* Then Zacchaeus had an idea. *I'll climb a tall tree. Then I can see Jesus!* Sitting high on a branch, he could see Jesus walking down the road.

As Jesus passed below, He stopped. Looking up into the tree He said, "Zacchaeus, come down. I will stay at your house today." That day Jesus told Zacchaeus the good news about God's forgiveness. And Zacchaeus gave his life to God.

Jesus wants us to know Him.

Zacchaeus wanted to know Jesus.

I won't let anything keep me from knowing Jesus.

Zacchaeus

Zacchaeus was a wee little man
A wee little man was he
He climbed up in a sycamore tree
For the Lord he wanted to see
And as the Savior passed that way
He looked up in the tree
And he said,
"Zacchaeus, you come down,
For I'm going to your house today!
For I'm going to your house today!"

Jesus, Our King

Matthew 21:1–9; Mark 11:1–10; Luke 19:28–38; John 12:12–15

The people of Jerusalem were excited. Jesus was coming! They had heard His wonderful stories, and they had seen His amazing miracles.

As Jesus rode on a donkey to Jerusalem, a huge crowd stood along the road. They began to sing and shout. Many people spread their coats across the road before Him. Some waved palm branches as if to welcome a king! Together they shouted, "Hosanna to the King! Blessed is He who comes in the name of the Lord!" Yes, Jesus was coming. What a happy time it was!

It is good to praise Jesus.

All of Jerusalem praised Jesus.

I will sing and shout praises to Jesus, my King.

Sing Hosanna!

Give me joy in my heart
Keep me singing
Give me joy in my heart, I pray (Hallelujah!)
Give me joy in my heart
Keep me singing
Keep me singing till the break of day

Sing hosanna, sing hosanna
Sing hosanna to the King of Kings
Sing hosanna, sing hosanna
Sing hosanna to the King

An Excellent Offering

Mark 12:41–44; Luke 21:1–4

In Bible times, people went to the temple to worship God. Near the door was a money box where people put their offerings. One day Jesus came to the temple. He sat near the money box and watched. He saw rich people put bags of coins into the box. The He saw a poor woman drop only two small coins into the money box.

Jesus was impressed. He told His disciples the poor woman had given more to God than any of the rich people. She hadn't given the most money, but she had given all she had. She loved and trusted God.

Our offering shows God we trust Him.

The woman gave an offering to God.

I will give to God.

Trust and Obey

When we walk with the Lord
In the light of His Word
What a glory He sheds on our way
While we do His good will
He abides with us still
And with all who will trust and obey

Trust and obey
For there's no other way
To be happy in Jesus
But to trust and obey

Serving Others

John 13:1–17

One evening Jesus and His disciples were eating dinner. Jesus taught them many things about God. Then He stood up and wrapped a towel around His waist. He kneeled down and began washing their feet. When He finished, He dried their feet with the towel.

Jesus said that to be like Him we must help others. "This is what a good helper does," He said. "Do as I am doing. Serve others. You will be happy if you do."

To be like Jesus, we must help others.

Jesus served His disciples by washing their feet.

I will help others to be like Jesus!

O How I Love Jesus

There is a name I love to hear
I love to sing its worth
It sounds like music to my ear
The sweetest name on earth

O how I love Jesus
O how I love Jesus
O how I love Jesus
Because He first loved me

Last Supper

Matthew 26:17–28; Mark 14:12–24; Luke 22:7–20; John 13:34–35

Jesus ate a special supper with His disciples. It was the last time He would eat with them. He told them many important things. Jesus took some bread and thanked God. He broke the bread and shared it with His disciples. Then He took a cup of wine and thanked God for it. He shared it too. He said, "Do this to remember Me."

Then He gave them a new rule. He told them, "Love each other. That's how people will know you love Me."

We show Jesus we love Him by loving others.

Jesus taught His disciples to love others.

I will love Jesus by loving others.

I Love Him Better Every D-A-Y

I love Him better every D-A-Y
I love Him better every D-A-Y
He is my Lord, the W-A-Y
I love Him better every D-A-Y

I love J-E-S-U-S
I know J-E-S-U-S
I need J-E-S-U-S
I love Him better every D-A-Y

The Way to Heaven

John 14:1–7

Jesus told His disciples He would soon leave to go to heaven. He told them not to worry. He was going to get a heavenly place ready for them. Then He would return and take them to their new heavenly home.

But Thomas said, "Lord, we don't know where You are going. How can we know the way?"

Jesus answered, "I am the way." Believing in Jesus leads us to heaven!

Jesus is preparing a place for us in heaven.

Thomas believed Jesus was the way to heaven.

I know Jesus is the only way to heaven.

Oh, You Can't Get to Heaven

Oh, you can't get to heaven on roller skates
'Cause you'd roll right by those pearly gates
Oh, you can't get to heaven on roller skates
'Cause you'd roll right by those pearly gates

Oh, you can't get to heaven in a rockin' chair
'Cause a rockin' chair won't get you there
Oh, you can't get to heaven in a rockin' chair
'Cause a rockin' chair won't get you there

Jesus Dies

Matthew 27:35–50; Mark 15:21–37;
Luke 23:33–49; John 19:17–37

It was a very sad day. The disciples did not know what to do. Mary was crying. They kept thinking about Jesus. They remembered all the wonderful things He had said and done. But today their hearts hurt. Soldiers put Jesus on a cross. They didn't believe He was God's Son. On the cross Jesus said, "My God, forgive them." Then He died.

Yes, it was a very sad day. But God wasn't finished. It was all in His plan to save us. In three days everything would change. His friends would soon be happy.

Jesus died so we might live.

Jesus forgave all our sins.

I am thankful Jesus died for me.

Praise Him 'Til the Sun Goes Down

Praise Him, praise Him
Praise Him in the morning
Praise Him in the noontime
Praise Him, praise Him
Praise Him 'til the sun goes down

Surprise—Jesus Is Alive!

Matthew 28:1–8; Mark 16:1–7;
Luke 24:1–12; John 20:1–18

After Jesus died, His friends buried Him in a cave called a tomb. Then they put a big stone in front to close it. But Jesus had a surprise for His friends.

When Mary went to the tomb where Jesus was buried, the stone had been rolled away. She saw two angels. They told her Jesus wasn't there. "He's alive!" they said.

Mary was so happy! She ran back to tell the disciples what she had seen. Jesus didn't stay dead! She told them, "Jesus is alive!"

Jesus is alive!

The tomb was empty!

I am happy that Jesus lives!

Christ the Lord Is Risen Today

Christ the Lord is risen today
Alleluia
Sons of men and angels say
Alleluia
Raise your joys and triumphs high
Alleluia
Sing, ye heavens, and earth, reply
Alleluia

A Big Catch

John 21:3–7

One day Peter, James, and John went fishing. They threw their nets into the water and waited. They fished all night but caught no fish.

In the morning, a man called from the shore, "Did you catch any fish?" When they told him they had not, He told them to throw their net on the right side of the boat. So they did. Suddenly, their net was full of fish!

Then Peter knew who the man on the shore was. "It's Jesus!" he said. Peter was so glad that he jumped into the water and swam to Jesus.

Jesus will help us in all we do.

He helped Peter, James, and John catch fish.

I know Jesus will help me too.

Peter, James, and John in a Sailboat

Peter, James, and John in a sailboat
Peter, James, and John in a sailboat
Peter, James, and John in a sailboat
Out on the deep blue sea

They fished all night, and they caught no fishes
Fished all night, and they caught no fishes
Fished all night, and they caught no fishes
Out on the deep blue sea

Jesus Goes to Heaven

Matthew 28:16–20; Mark 16:15–20; Luke 24:45–51; Acts 1:8–11

Jesus' work on earth was done. His followers had seen Him die on the cross and come alive again. Jesus told them they should go everywhere and tell people about Him. Then He said, "Now I am going to live with My Father."

His followers watched as Jesus rose up in the air until He disappeared into the clouds. His friends looked up into the sky for a long time. Someday Jesus will come back the same way the disciples saw Him leave.

Jesus is in heaven,

but He is coming again.

I will watch for Jesus to return.

J-E-S-U-S

To the tune of "B-I-N-G-O"

**There is a name I love to sing
And Jesus is His name-o
J-E-S-U-S, J-E-S-U-S, J-E-S-U-S
And Jesus is His name-o**

Tell the Good News

Matthew 28:16–20

Heaven is a happy place. That's why Jesus said, "Go to all the world and tell everyone the good news!" We should tell people who speak English. Tell those who speak Spanish. Tell those who speak Russian and Chinese too. This is a great big world, and there are lots of people. But everyone needs to know that God loves them.

That's great news! People who love Jesus will get to go to heaven someday. So let's tell everyone!

All people need to know about Jesus.

Jesus said to go and tell others about Him.

I will go and tell others about Jesus.

If You're Saved and You Know It

To the tune of "If You're Happy and You Know It"

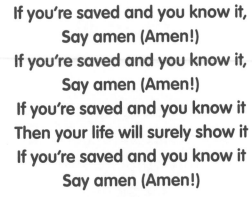

If you're saved and you know it,
Say amen (Amen!)
If you're saved and you know it,
Say amen (Amen!)
If you're saved and you know it
Then your life will surely show it
If you're saved and you know it
Say amen (Amen!)

Peter Heals the Beggar

Acts 3:1–10

Once a poor man sat by the temple gates. He couldn't walk, so there he sat, day after day, begging for money. One day Peter and John went to the temple. As they passed, the beggar cried out to Peter and John for money.

Peter said, "We don't have any money. But we will give you what we do have." Peter took the man's hand and the man stood, walked, and then jumped. His legs were well! Then Peter said, "It is Jesus' power that made you well." The man left praising God, and everyone was amazed.

It is good to share Jesus' love with others.

Peter and John shared God's love with a man who couldn't walk.

I will share the love of Jesus.

Silver and Gold

Peter and John went to pray
They met a lame man on the way
He asked for alms and held out his palms
And this is what Peter did say

Silver and gold have I none
But such as I have give I thee
In the name of Jesus Christ of Nazareth
Rise up and walk

Saul Sees the Light

Acts 9:1–18

Jesus is the Son of God. People who believe this are called Christians. Saul didn't believe that Jesus was the Son of God. He went from city to city putting Christians in prison.

One day as he was traveling on the road to Damascus, a bright light shined down on him. It was so bright that it blinded him. Then Saul heard a voice from heaven saying, "Saul, why are you so unkind to Me?"

Saul asked, "Who are you?"

The voice answered, "I am Jesus." Then Saul believed in Jesus, and his life was changed forever.

Jesus can change your life.

Saul learned that Jesus is God, and then he obeyed Jesus.

I will obey Jesus. I will be a Christian!

Walking with Jesus

Walking with Jesus
Walking every day, all along the way
For I am walking with Jesus
Walking with Jesus alone

Walking with Jesus
(Walking in the sunlight, walking in the shadow)
Walking every day, all along the way
For I am walking with Jesus
(Walking in the sunlight, walking in the shadow)
Walking with Jesus alone

Paul and Silas in Prison

Acts 16:19–25; Romans 8:28

Have you ever received a letter from someone? Letters can bring good news. Saul, who was also known as Paul, wrote letters to Christians, and they were full of good news. Paul wrote that no matter what bad things happened to Jesus' followers, God was working for their good.

Paul and Silas were once put in prison for doing good things. But even when they were locked in chains, they were happy. They knew that God was working for their good. We know that God is always helping people who love Him. That's very good!

In all that happens, God is working for our good.

Even when Paul and Silas were in prison, God was working for their good.

I believe that God is working to help me.

Paul and Silas

To the tune of "Do Lord"

Paul and Silas bound in jail all night long
Paul and Silas bound in jail all night long
Paul and Silas bound in jail all night long
Saying, "Who shall deliver me?"

Paul and Silas prayed to God all night long
Paul and Silas prayed to God all night long
Paul and Silas prayed to God all night long
Saying, "Who shall deliver me?"

God's Grace

Romans 10:9, 13; Ephesians 2:8

The sound of a siren is a scary sound. It means danger. But the sound of a bird singing is sweet to our ears. The sound of popcorn popping is sweet to our mouths. But to our hearts, there's nothing sweeter than the sound of the word *grace*.

Paul wrote about grace in the Bible. Grace has a very simple meaning: God forgives us no matter what we've said or done. All we have to do is ask Him! God offers grace to everyone. He has grace for you and grace for me. God's grace is truly amazing!

God's grace is amazing!

He will forgive us for the bad things we do.

Thank You, God, for Your grace to me!

If We Ever

If we ever needed the Lord before
We sure do need Him now
Oh, we sure do need Him now
Oh, Lord, we sure do need Him now
If we ever needed the Lord before
We sure do need Him now
We need Him every day and every hour

God's Great Big Love!

Ephesians 3:18–19

It's easy to measure the size of this book. All you need is a ruler. It's easy to measure the length of a long train or measure the height of the tallest person. We can even measure the tallest building and the widest ocean.

But who can measure how big God's love is? It's higher than the highest star and wider than the east is from the west. It fills the heavens from end to end. We can't measure it, but we can treasure it!

God's love is big!

God's love fills the heavens and the earth.

I am thankful for God's love.

Deep and Wide

Deep and wide, deep and wide
There's a fountain flowing deep and wide
Deep and wide, deep and wide
There's a fountain flowing deep and wide

Working for Jesus

Colossians 3:23

Some jobs can be lots of fun. Helping Dad wash the car is fun. Helping Mom bake a cake is fun too. But some jobs are not much fun. Cleaning your room can be boring. Picking up dirty socks can be awful.

But Paul wrote in the Bible that whether a job is fun or not, you should do your very best. You should work as if you were washing God's car or baking God a cake or even picking up God's socks. Always do your best!

God wants us to do our best.

Jesus always did His best.

I will always do my best!

When the Roll Is Called Up Yonder

Let us labor for the Master
From the dawn till setting sun
Let us talk of all His wondrous love and care
Then when all of life is over
And our work on earth is done
And the roll is called up yonder
I'll be there

When the roll is called up yonder
When the roll is called up yonder
When the roll is called up yonder
When the roll is called up yonder
I'll be there

195

The Bible Is True

2 Timothy 3:14–16

Paul wrote a letter to his friend Timothy. In it he said that all the verses in the Bible are true and that it's important to learn them.

God gave us the Bible to teach us how to live good lives that honor Him. It tells us that Jesus is God's Son and is the Savior of the world. It teaches us to treat other people with kindness and love and to help other people whenever we can. It even shows us the way to heaven. Yes, the Bible is a very special book. It is God's Word!

The Bible is a special book from God.

God's Word is true.

I will read my Bible and know it is true.

The B-I-B-L-E

The B-I-B-L-E
Yes, that's the book for me
I stand alone on the Word of God
The B-I-B-L-E

Jesus Is Knocking

Revelation 3:20

Knock, knock, knock! Have you ever heard that sound? Of course you have! It's the sound of someone knocking on a door. When you hear that sound, you go to the door to see who is knocking.

Jesus once said that your heart is like a door. He stands at the door of your heart and knocks. Jesus loves you and wants you to invite Him into your heart. If you feel Jesus knocking, let Him in!

Jesus wants you to invite Him in.

Jesus knocks on the door of your heart.

I will invite Jesus to come into my heart.

Behold, Behold

Behold, behold
I stand at the door and knock, knock, knock
Behold, behold
I stand at the door and knock, knock, knock
If anyone hears my voice
If anyone hears my voice
And will open, open, open the door
I will come in

Heaven

Revelation 21–22

The Bible says that heaven is a very special place. It's special because it is God's home! All of the angels live there too. The streets there are made of gold and shine like glass. A heavenly river is there with water as clear as crystal. The gates of heaven are made of beautiful pearls. The walls shine with jewels. But most importantly, Jesus is there!

People who love and trust in Jesus will meet Him there. We will walk and talk with Him. We will share His love and joy forever in heaven. Heaven is a wonderful place!

God made heaven for those He loves.

Jesus lives in heaven.

I love Jesus so I will live forever with Him.

When We All Get to Heaven

Sing the wondrous love of Jesus
Sing His mercy and His grace
In the mansions bright and blessed
He'll prepare for us a place

When we all get to heaven
What a day of rejoicing that will be
When we all see Jesus
We'll sing and shout the victory